FOREWORD

The Crowther Centre Monographs
aiming to promote missiological research at a serious yet accessible level. These will be occasional publications addressing current issues in mission. They aim not only to inform but also to transform as writers present a summary of the implications of their research.

We hope that as various issues in mission are explored in this series, they will challenge and enhance not only our understanding of God, but also our engagement with God's world. Missiology, or the study of issues in mission, is an applied and engaged discipline. It is a discipline that encourages us to be active and involved so that we live out a theology of the road rather than one of the balcony. Missiology also draws on other disciplines – it is wide ranging and eclectic as it seeks to understand the implications of working out God's mission in an increasingly complex and globalised world. And finally, missiology is an incomplete discipline – as it seeks to reflect on the practice of mission, it will always be developing. So there is no such thing as a definitive missiology – there is only missiology in progress.

May you enjoy and be challenged as you read these essays and may they open up new vistas and expanding horizons for you as you journey in God's mission in the world today.

DR CATHY ROSS
MANAGER FOR CROWTHER CENTRE FOR MISSION EDUCATION

Trauma, Migration and Mission: Biblical Reflections from a traumatized Hebrew

Dr Ida Glaser was Missiologist-in-Residence at CMS from October 2007 to March 2008. She gave this paper at the official opening of the Crowther Centre for Mission Education on 4 December 2007.

Trauma is a Greek word, meaning 'wound'. We know that it has to do with mission because the one place it appears in the New Testament is in Jesus' exposition of the commandment to love our neighbours: it was into the trauma of the beaten Jew that the Good Samaritan poured his oil and wine (Luke 10.34). The word also appears as a verb, *traumatizo*, twice: first, in the parable of the wicked tenants who traumatize the third emissary from their master (Luke 20.12), and second in Acts 19.16, when the sons of Sceva are traumatized by the man with the evil spirit. The world, it seems, is a dangerous place, where human beings can wound us if we do our mission in God's way, and evil powers can wound us if we do it in our own way. The missionary is called to minister to the traumatized, but our shared humanity means that she is also in danger of trauma, and the missionary calling increases the danger.

It is not surprising, then, that all the synoptic gospels record Jesus preparing His disciples for potentially traumatic events coming in both the near and the distant future –: the fall of Jerusalem; the wars, famines and natural disasters of the end times; and the persecutions that will beset His followers throughout (Matthew 24, Mark 13, Luke 21). One of the results of such events is that people become refugees: Jesus even advises His disciples to become refugees (Matthew 24.16, Mark 13.14, Luke 21.21). Embedded in these chapters are key statements on mission:

- "This gospel of the kingdom will be proclaimed throughout the whole world as a testimony to all nations, and then the end will come." (Matthew 24.14)
- "The gospel must first be proclaimed to all nations . . say whatever is given you in that hour, for it is not you who speak but the Holy Spirit." (Mark 13.10-11)
- "This will be an opportunity for you to bear witness." (Luke 21.13).

The juxtaposition of traumatic events, flight and mission in these chapters provides the impetus for offering this paper.

Migration is often associated with trauma. It can be voluntary or involuntary, by choice or by necessity. If involuntary, the migration is likely to have been caused by traumatic events, and the very process of displacement can have traumatic dimensions even for voluntary migrants[1]. The nexus of mission with migration is therefore likely to necessitate dealing with trauma: this paper focuses on biblical resources for doing so.

1 This can be especially so for children of people who chose to migrate. See for example, Eva Hoffman, *Lost in Translation: A Life in a New Language*, London: Heinemann, 1989.

I distinguish here between 'trauma' and 'traumatic events'. By 'trauma', I shall mean a kind of wounding that can result from experiencing, witnessing or even hearing about 'traumatic events': that is, situations of acute danger which a person is powerless to resist. Such events usually result in loss and consequent grief for all; but the occurrence, nature and extent of trauma as defined below depends on numerous factors.

My research methodology has been a year struggling with Post Traumatic Shock Disorder following a head injury which triggered traumatic memories from the car accident in which my parents and grandfather were killed when I was 15 years old; and five and a half decades of learning to cope with being the daughter of a Jew who took two years to travel from Czechoslovakia to the UK during the Second World War, and with bearing the name of my father's mother who died in Auschwitz. It is, if you like, a very personalized case study. It is how a particular individual with a particular history of personal, family and ethnic experience of trauma and migration has been reading scripture.[2]

1. Trauma and recovery[3]

In English, and particularly in medicine and psychology, the word 'trauma' has developed specific meanings. I want now to explore the understanding of trauma as a state resulting from an experience that combines extreme danger with utter helplessness. Such trauma has physiological as well as psychological dimensions, because of the way that the body responds to danger: it produces adrenalin. It seems that the combination of danger and helplessness can lead to the adrenalin being unable to find its normal release, so something gets stuck. Instead of the mind and body processing the horrible event in the normal way:

- The body, through the autonomic nervous system, gets stuck in its responses to stimuli associated with the event – summarized as fight, flight or freeze.
- The mind keeps repeating the memory – whether at a conscious or sub-conscious level. You see the thing happening again and again in dreams or in 'flashbacks', and, when it's really acute, it is like living in it.
- Mind and body are constantly anticipating a repeat of the events. The body can be in a state of constant arousal, which may be evidenced in 'startle responses' – uncontrollable jerks in response to any stimulus that suggests the original traumatic situation.

In summary, we might say that the event is experienced in the present (in repeated

2 If it appears a little fragmented, that is because trauma tends to fragmentize one's thinking!

3 This section owes much of its understanding of the dynamics of trauma to J. Herman, *Trauma and Recovery: The Aftermath of Violence – From Domestic Abuse to Political Terror*, NY: Basic Books, 1992.

memories) and in the future (in constant anticipation of a repeat) instead of, as is normal with memories, in the past. Through it all is the sense of DANGER and HELPLESSNESS. There is likely to be a constant struggle for safety and control to compensate for these feelings. There may also be a variety of physical and mental symptoms – sleeplessness, weight change, nausea, irritability, and feelings of dissociation, fragmentation and disconnection. Very common is what is sometimes called 'survivor guilt' – feeling that you are somehow responsible for what happened or for not averting it, or that you rather than others should have died. Some people even feel that they have died, or no longer exist. Some compensate by trying to achieve great things in order to justify their survival.

All this applies very widely, consciously or unconsciously, at both personal and communal levels: the children of refugees live with an edge of fear and their reactions are dominated by 'fight', 'flight' or 'freeze'; communities feeling under threat play the 'terrorist outrage' over and over on TV. Again and again in traumatized communities, we see desperate 'it must never happen again' attempts to escape danger, and their members fight to convince themselves that they are not really helpless.

Such trauma is often resistant to ordinary talk-based counselling techniques. It cannot effectively be dealt with until whatever has been stuck gets unstuck. There are various strategies that can be used to access the memories so that they can be processed and the experience can move into the past.[4] The body can then be re-trained to change its responses to the remembered stimuli.

Herman proposes three stages on the journey to recovery which must, she says, take place within the context of relationships, and must involve the recognition that recovery does not depend on someone else putting things right.[5] These stages are:

1 establishing a sense of safety;

2 recovering and processing memories;

3 reconnecting with the world as a survivor.

These three stages can be discerned in the biblical material explored below. The importance of healing relationships which can be offered by the church, the missionary and, most importantly, by God Himself through Christ, is assumed.

---

4 See, for example, F. Shapiro and M.S. Silk, *EMDR: The Breakthrough Therapy for Overcoming Anxiety, Stress and Trauma*, NY: Basic Books, 1997; L. Heller and D.P. Heller, *Crash Course: Auto Accident Recovery Breakthrough,* Berkeley, California: North Atlantic Books, 2001.

5 This is a logical progression, but the stages are not discrete: they can be variously traversed in time.

2. Getting started

2.1 Seeing trauma in the Bible

I have found analyzing trauma along two axes a helpful starting point for seeking relevant biblical material:

2.1.1 Between trauma caused by events originating in human sin, and trauma caused by events originating in the natural order.

In Matthew 24, events originating in human sin would include persecutions and wars. Events originating in the natural order would include earthquakes and famines. There are numerous other places in the Bible that deal with either 'natural disaster' or human atrocities. There is, however, a spectrum here. We now recognize that many apparently natural disasters have been aggravated or even caused by human agency – whether by environmental damage, by factors leading to the vulnerability of the victims, or by deliberate or accidental mishandling of the aftermath of the events.

Where does a car crash fit along this axis? On the one hand, we call it an 'accident', implying an uncontrollable chance, and therefore, perhaps, a 'natural' event. On the other hand, my father was driving the car when he was tired, and someone had left a lorry parked in the wrong place. It seems to me that such an event is therefore situated right at the centre of the axis, along with events caused by other man-made devices that unwittingly let loose the destructive powers of nature. The greatest potential for trauma is when human attempts to control the natural order are directed towards evil ends; but there can also be enormous damage when human beings find their attempts loosing powers beyond their control.

2.1.2 Between individual and ethnic trauma.

There is **individual trauma**: each person's experience is different, and such specific trauma symptoms as referred to above depend on particular experiences. For example, although my brother also survived the car crash, the head injury with the resultant memory loss and the recent similar injury that triggered the lost memories was mine alone.

There is **trauma that affects families** – nuclear and extended. Even a trauma that apparently affects only one person – for example, a rape that is not spoken of – affects family and friends because it affects the person's relationships with them. In our case, the death of my parents resulted in the immediate immigration of my father's sister and her children from the Czech Republic. In addition to the shock of loss there was the change of place, culture and language for the immigrating family, and the change of language and culture within the home for the receiving family.

There is **trauma that affects whole communities and ethnic groups**. For example, the 'holocaust' affects not only our family but also all Jews, whether or not their families were directly involved, and to whichever post-'holocaust' generation they belong. To this can be added the whole history of Jewish experience under hostile rule.

There is **trauma with world-wide effects**. This can be through media coverage, or simply because the events are so extensive that they affect the course of history and/or are so terrible that many countries and peoples get involved. There are obvious recent examples, but I would also include the 'holocaust' here, with its lasting heritage of publicity and guilt, and the political ramifications of seeking security for future generations.

The Bible deals with individual trauma in, for example, Job, various Psalms, and stories of individuals. However, all this is embedded in the history of Israel, and in the documents of the early Christian community. This paper arises out of immediate individual trauma, but it has the background of family and communal contexts and is undergirded by the conviction that family and community are fundamental to dealing with individual trauma as with everything else.

A key biblical resource is the often traumatic experience of the Jewish people. The word 'Hebrew' may or may not originate as a somewhat derogatory term for slaves and migrants, but the condition of exile and humiliation is a frequent one in Jewish history – in both biblical and post-biblical times. I have written elsewhere of the use of Psalm 137 as a place for processing memories of peoples traumatized by conflict and land loss.[6] The Psalm invites readers into the experience of Israel, thus normalising the trauma and dealing with consequent grief, anger and isolation. Part of the condition of trauma is often a feeling of isolation and difference: hence the importance of sufferers understanding that they share the experience with others.

2.2 Two key concepts

2.2.1 The normality of trauma

Our 21st century western world breeds the myth that safety is the normal human condition, which occasionally gets violated by dangers that someone ought to avert. Biblically, there is a measure of truth in this, in that God created a good and safe world, so this is what we long for. However, safety disappeared very rapidly as sin appeared, and the hard facts are that danger is now normal, and that we are often powerless to counter it. It is not only that such feelings as those expressed in Psalm 137 are normal responses to violence and exile, it is also that traumatic events are, since the 'fall', the regular human experience.

So, in Matthew 24, Mark 13 and Luke 21, Jesus tells his disciples to be ready for

6 'We sat down and wept: Biblical resources for conflict situations', in *The Round Table: The Commonwealth Journal of International Affairs,* Issue 382, 2005, pp 641-52.

traumatic events. He prepares them both for traumatic events due to human sin and for traumatic events due to natural causes. The teaching can be applied by individuals, but is addressed to a group. In summary, he taught that:

- traumatic events are to be expected;
- they are meaningful – in terms of mission, of judgement, and of the eschaton, which is the ultimate aim of the world;
- they are limited – both in intensity and in duration;
- In the midst of them, there is something that will never pass away, so that:
- the person who endures to the end will be SAFE.

Underlying all is the assurance that, despite all appearances, God and only God is in control. He and only he knows (v36).

There are two corollaries here for mission.

First, it offers a resource for ministry to people involved in traumatic events. The acknowledgement of the commonality and normality of trauma can help to deal with the disconnection, isolation and anger that so often follows traumatic experience. The assurances of meaning and limitation give hope. The vision of something permanent offers a fixed point of reference in an apparently chaotic world. Safety and control are, as we shall see, crucial.

Second, if we take this teaching seriously and prepare ourselves to face such events, they will become for us opportunities for witness (Luke 21.13), for sharing in the proclamation of the Kingdom of God (Matthew 24.14). How? In the place of helplessness, we will find the Holy Spirit, the promised helper, speaking through us (Mark 13.11). The place of trauma becomes the place of mission.

2.2.2 Safety and control

> 'The core experiences of psychological trauma are disempowerment and disconnection from others. Recovery, therefore, is based upon the empowerment of the survivor and the creation of new connections.'[7]

The biblical resources explored in section 3 below take up the themes of empowerment and reconnection. However, there is a prior requisite: Herman's first stage of recovery is establishing a place of safety. The books tell us that, in order to start processing the traumatic memory and let it recede into the past,

7 J. Herman, *Trauma and Recovery: The aftermath of violence – from domestic abuse to political terror*, NY: Basic Books, 1992, p133. This section owes much of its understanding of the dynamics of trauma to Herman.

- the feeling of danger needs to be countered by being in a place of safety, and
- the feeling of helplessness needs to be countered by being in control.

From a biblical perspective, these are forlorn efforts: the world is fallen and therefore not a safe place; and trying to be in control is the original sin. I want to agree that safety and control are of key importance in dealing with a condition rooted in danger and helplessness, but to suggest that God is the only one who can safely be in control, and that the only ultimate safety is in God himself – and that is a safety that can face even the dreaded repeat of the traumatic event, because it lasts beyond death. Of course, finding as much physical safety as possible, and the realization that one is responsible for one's own recovery and not a helpless victim, are still necessary. However, the recognition of God as the place of safety and control both offers ultimate security and puts self-control into perspective.

There is a mass of biblical material on God as the author of safety (related words are often translated in terms of 'salvation') in both this world and the next. Here, I want to focus briefly on God as a PLACE of safety, before going on to the next section which takes up the theme of God in control. As the worship song says, quoting Proverbs 18.10, 'The name of the Lord is a strong tower: the righteous runs into it and he is *SAFE*.'

One of the rabbinic names for God is '*Ha Maqqom*' – 'The Place'. The idea is explored in the Midrash on Genesis 28.10[8], where Jacob, setting out for Haran, 'came to a certain place' (ESV). In the understanding of this midrash, Jacob met the *shekinah*, and it is to the *shekinah* that the Torah refers in the word 'place'. Why? Because God is the Place of the world. The train of thought then moves to the 'place near God' in the cleft of the rock, where Moses could safely stand as the glory passed (Exodus 33.21-2), and to God as dwelling-place (*ma'on*) in Deuteronomy 33.27 and Psalm 90.1. The question underlying this *midrash* is whether God is the dwelling-place of the world, or the world is the dwelling-place of God; and conclusion is that the world is in God and not vice versa. The Christian might move further, to the *shekinah* dwelling in the world in Christ, and recall that *Yeshua*, the Hebrew name for 'Jesus', can be translated 'safety'.

One of the techniques for processing traumatic memories is to return repeatedly to an envisaged place of safety. The idea of God as The Place in which the world dwells, and therefore as the dwelling place of God's people and of the individual, indicates a truly safe place.

Midrash often gathers together references to similar ideas from different parts of the Bible. Before the discussion of '*Ha Maqqom*', the Midrash here applies Proverbs 3.24

8 *Genesis Rabbah* 48:9

to Jacob, and puts Psalm 121 into his mouth.[9] As he comes to lie down in the Place, God's promise to those who observe his wisdom is applied to him: 'You will go your way safely and not injure your feet. When you lie down you will be unafraid; you will lie down and your sleep will be sweet. You will not fear the sudden terror or the disaster that comes upon the wicked, for the Lord will be your trust; he will keep your feet from being caught' (JPS translation). He responds with the assurance that, helpless though Jacob is in himself, God is his helper and his protector from all that he fears. Jacob's sense of helplessness is not countered by a sense of his being in control, but by the assurance that help will come from the Lord who is in control.

It is crucial to the above understanding that God's control is, ultimately, safe.[10] In fact, he is the only one who can safely take control, because he is the only one who has both complete goodness and complete wisdom. His control deals with both ends of our first trauma spectrum: he made the natural order, and his management of potentially destructive forces is without the weakness of human limitation or the taint of human sin.

It is this God who is the safe place, the helper of the helpless.

3. Biblical resources 1: Empowerment - God in control.

The corollary of the above, and the thesis that underlies what follows, is that empowerment must be rooted in perception of God's control, and of his infinite goodness and wisdom. It is not an empowerment dependent on achieving safety, or on struggling to take control over the dangerous thing. It is based on the hard acknowledgement that there really are areas in which we are helpless, but there is a helper, who can help us stand on our own two feet and move forward. It is an empowerment found in trust, in the acceptance both of our limitation and of our value as having been made in his image, in knowing forgiveness of sin, and in accepting the help of the Holy Spirit.

The idea of this God being in control has been the single most important idea in helping me through the past year. Here follow three biblical resources that have been most helpful.

3.1 Noah

There can be few worse experiences than having the whole world and its peoples destroyed around you; but I have found the flood story an essential foundation,

9 *Genesis Rabbah* 48:1-2.

10 The rabbis recognise that this is not always apparent, and that it often appears that the righteous suffer more than the wicked. *Genesis Rabbah* 48:5 notes that apparent ease of Esau and suffering of Jacob at this time, and observes: 'Thus we learn that the Holy One, blessed be He, hastens the happiness of the wicked and delays that of the righteous.'

because it shows God in control BOTH of human sin and of the natural order.

- God is in control of nature. In fact, he is able to un-make and re-make it all, because he is its creator. In particular, he is in control of the waters, which represented fearsome forces of destruction to the peoples of the time.
- God is in control of human wickedness. The Noah story can be read as Genesis' response to the question of human evil.

This would be terrifying if it were presented as God's normal mode of action – he would be the author of trauma. But the point of the Noah story is that God has covenanted never to destroy like this again. God's control is subject to the promise of preservation of the natural order until the eschaton.

There is, of course, a problem here. What does it MEAN that God is in control of a world that contains traumatic events? Were the people who did unspeakable things to my grandmother somehow doing his will? Was my family particularly under God's judgement? I am not going to try to solve such problems, but to offer some pointers that I have found helpful in living with the questions. Essentially, the flood and the covenant together sum up God's response to human wickedness. It is most important here to notice how the Genesis writer locates both the decision to destroy and the decision to preserve in the very heart of God. In both chapter 6 (v5) and chapter 8 (v21), we read that the human heart is thoroughly wicked. In both, God reflects in his heart. The first time, he decides to destroy: the second, because of the aroma of Noah's sacrifice, he covenants never to do so again.

The decision to preserve is linked with the aroma of the sacrifice. Christians recognize this as an early pointer to the cross – the place where human wickedness is dealt with by God Himself, so that human beings can find forgiveness and, as it were, an ark in which to find safety from the flood.

Here is good news for the many who, whether because of religious teaching or personal reactions, fear that the traumatic event was a judgement; and also for those who feel guilty about their responses to it, or for whom self-blame is one of the 'stuck' responses to trauma triggers. Any real guilt can be forgiven.

Noah and his family were saved in the ark by God's grace (6.8): Noah says nothing but simply obeys God. Here are two helpful pictures for those who are, or feel, surrounded by danger: an ark in which to live safely through the storm, and an oasis of quiet obedience in the midst of a tumultuous world.

The decision to judge is not out of a detached or angry desire to destroy, but out of a heart of GRIEF (6.6). The word translated 'pain' or 'grief' is *'itsvon'*. The root of this is used to mean "The most intense form of human emotion, a mixture of rage and bitter anguish".[11] It is used of God elsewhere in the Old Testament only in Psalm 78.40 and Is 63.10, to describe his agonizing over the rebellion of his beloved Israel. Its intensity can be seen from its use in relation to human beings: Dinah's brothers, when they heard of her rape (Genesis 34.7); Joseph's brothers, confronted with the brother they had wronged (Genesis 45.5); Jonathan, when Saul wanted to kill David (1 Samuel 20.34); David, when he heard of Absalom's death (2 Samuel 19.3); and a deserted wife (Isaiah 54.6).

The root has already been used four times in Genesis – in 5.29, 3.16 (twice) and 3.17. In each case, it refers to the pain that both women and men suffer because of the fall. 3.16 and 17 are part of the 'curses', and 5.29 tells of the longing of Noah's father to have some relief from the painful toil of the very long lives lived by his ancestors.

Putting all this together, we can suggest both that the divine heart mirrors the pain and grief experienced by his image as a result of sin and that our sense of grief and outrage at traumatic events can mirror God's own response to them. Rabbinic comment on Genesis 6.6 sees Ecclesiastes 2.21-22 as describing God's grief over the way that humans have handled his creation, and underlines this by citing Genesis 7v10 and the use *'itsvon* to describe David's grief for Absalom as evidence that God took the full seven days of mourning for a near relative over his creation before sending the flood.[12] The pain in the heart of the God who is in control and who accepts the sacrifice is what, for me, makes the existence of trauma bearable.

Psalm 46, offers a helpful meditation on some of these ideas. Natural disasters are dealt with in v2-3: we need not fear if the waters are raging again, and the earth appears to be falling apart. Human-caused disasters are dealt with in v 6 and 8-10: it is God who judges, who ends warfare, and who says, 'Desist! I dominate the nations! I dominate the earth!' (JPS translation). In the centre of the psalm is a reflection on this God being in the midst of his people; the first and last verses declare him to be a refuge, a stronghold and a haven. For the traumatized, overwhelmed by helplessness, perhaps the most telling verses are one and five. God, being 'very near' and 'in the midst', is the help in trouble, the One coming to help. Our God is the God of Jacob.

The more common translation of v8 is also telling: 'Be still and know that I am God!' It is not only that the nations should heed God and stop fighting, but that the wounded can be still in the knowledge that God is the one fighting the battles. This is an invitation into the ark of safety in God's presence, but also a challenge to endure the long, slow journey through the incapacity caused by the trauma.

---

11 G. Wenham, *Genesis 1-15*, Waco, Texas: Word Books, 1987, p144

12 *Genesis Rabbah* 27: 1-4, 32: 7.

3.2 Job

The book that most obviously explores individual trauma is Job – and the tragedies that beset him apparently originated both with human beings (the Sabaeans and Chaldeans who attacked his oxen, donkeys and camels) and with natural disaster (the fire that destroyed the sheep and shepherds, and the wind that killed his children). Thus Job deals with both ends of our trauma spectrum as well as with Job's own personal discomfort.

Most of the book deals with Job's agonies and questionings, and with the inadequacy of human response. I want to focus here on something that Job found totally adequate: God's speaking to him out of the whirlwind. There are doubtless many ways of hearing God's response to Job. Until recently, I had found it easy enough to identify with Job's laments, but had tended to hear the same harsh tones in God's words as in those of the 'comforters'. It is only through the past year's experience that I have begun to understand how Job could have been satisfied with both the manner and the content of God's response.

Job had been speaking to his friends, and they to him for 35 chapters. He has been through suicidal despair to anger, tried to make sense of it all, argued about justice, glimpsed a possible resolution after death, and then turned to lamenting his losses. But, by the end of all this, his distress was unallayed. This was not only because his friends were insensitive counsellors, or because they got their theology wrong. The Septuagint uses 'trauma' to translate *'k'eb'* in Job 16.6:

> *If I speak, my trauma is not assuaged,*
> *and if I forbear, how much of it leaves me?*

Job thinks that he could comfort the comforters were their positions reversed (16.1-6), but there is something in his own pain that cannot be reached by speaking. The passage goes on to describe the agony of feeling that God is the enemy who is tearing him apart; and Job's final words in 31.35-40 are a plea for something more than words. Where Elihu offers only words, God's response in chapters 38-41 is satisfactory because it goes far beyond mere speech.

Most obviously, this is **a direct encounter with God**. A key here is 42.5: Job is at last able to rest because he has received an answer direct from God, which is what he wanted all along. The 'comforters' had already told him about God's control, and, as chapter 16 suggests, his knowledge that God was in control was a major part of Job's problem. Telling Job that God was in control just made matters worse: he needed to hear God for himself. The personal encounter allows him to hear what we may not hear by reading chapters 38-40 – the tone of God's voice, as it were. Where the 'comforters' exposition of God's control was one of judgement, God's own voice spoke affirmation as well as challenge and reminded Job of his human dignity (38.3, 40.7). The outcome was also much more than speech – it was a total reversal of his condition.

For the traumatized, a key observation is that God spoke to Job **out of the whirlwind**. The scene is an approaching storm, with a background of rumbling thunder (v2). Elihu is telling Job that God is in control of the weather – for judgement and for blessing. Given his previous experience, this was not something that Job needed to be told. If he was traumatized by the wind's destruction of his children, then the approach of the wind must have triggered a sense of impending doom. Together with Elihu's message of judgement, it would have been terrifying. However, we find that it is out of the very destructive forces that caused the trauma that God speaks. Facing the terror and meeting God there is the key to unlocking the trauma.

- Facing the terror is necessary to 'unsticking' whatever got stuck in the original traumatic event. Only then can the memories begin to be processed.
- Meeting God there gives an experience of positive survival in the face of the danger. It is a step on the way to 'desensitization' – to re-training the system so that it responds more positively to what have hitherto been trauma triggers.
- For Job, the meeting with God culminated in his being given a job – praying for his friends – and in restoration of what had been lost. The whole negative experience was limited in time, and had a positive outcome.

Job did not realize it, but the gathering storm was a sign of God's coming. Henceforward, he would be able to perceive the wind as a herald of God rather than of disaster.

To turn my attention to God in the face of my various trauma triggers – to find THERE a security in his greatness and my smallness, to heed THERE the call to stand straight in my human dignity – is an ongoing challenge; but it is a great help in the long journey of desensitization. What can God say to me in traffic noise? I have heard him say, 'You survived! You are here! You are here because I want you here: I didn't let you die or even be critically injured.'

Finally, **what did God say to Job**? The main message is loud and clear: it is the message that I have suggested is so crucial to the traumatized, that God is in control of both human evil and the natural order. Chapters 38-41 speak first of the weather and then of the animals, but also of God's judging human beings. The control over weather and animals in chapters 38 and 39 serves the preliminary purpose of stilling Job: he sees how big God is and how small[13] he is, and can be quiet and listen (40.4). The declaration of God's justice and the demonstration of the limitations of human justice with its implications of the ineffectiveness of human anger in 40.8-14, followed by the

13 This is the root meaning of the word translated 'unworthy' (NIV) or 'of small account' (ESV).

poem of God's control over the monsters, enables Job to worship (42.6).

It is interesting that the **form** of this message is that of God questioning Job. Trauma puts everything into question, so it is not surprising that, hitherto, Job has been questioning God and his friends and everything around him. But the deepest pain, underlying the rage and confusion, is likely to be that trauma puts the self into question. The experience disrupts my whole way of being, and leaves me feeling disconnected and fragmented. So Job's encounter with God turns into a call to encounter himself. 'Who is this?' (38v2) may refer to Elihu, who 'darkened counsel with words without knowledge', but Job refers it to himself in 42.3. By the end, he realizes that his problems will not be solved by reforming his comforters, but by his own humble acceptance of whatever God permits. He knew that in the beginning (1.20-21), but now he knows it in a whole new way.

God's only instruction to Job, repeated in 31.3 and 40.7, is to stand up as a human being in order to hear God's questions. Before he is reminded of God's greatness, Job is reminded that, as a human being made in God's image, he can stand and meet God. It is thus, standing, that God gives him, as it were, a tour of creation, and he knows himself as a small creature. At last,he sees God's greatness and accepts his own limitations, and that is why he can stop his agonized but ineffective speech.

There is relief in acknowledging my smallness. The world is NOT going to collapse if I am too traumatized to function. I'm not in charge – God is. So it doesn't matter too much if I don't understand what's going on. All I really need to know is that God is in control, and that he is good.

There is joy in understanding myself in the context of creation – in having survived to see its beauty, in recognizing that God cares for it and controls it, and in knowing that he values me, small as I am, more than the sparrows.

There is liberation I knowing that my path to wholeness depends on myself before God, and not on any other human being. It does not depend on anyone who has wronged me making amends, or on any 'comforter' getting things right. It is myself I need to meet, and I can do that as I meet God, accept all that has happened to me, and offer it back to him.

3.3 Revelation

Much of the New Testament is written out of or into situations of migration, persecution or even famine. The book that deals most explicitly with such issues is, perhaps, Revelation: it is written from enforced exile and, like Jesus in Matthew 24, Mark 13 and Luke 21, it focuses both on opposition to discipleship and on the traumatic events of the end times. And, as in these chapters, the accomplishment of the mission to the nations is embedded in the treatment of these concerns (e.g. 5.9, 7.9, 11.9, 14.6ff,

15.4, 17.15, 21.24, 22.2). It is not surprising, then, that the main features of Jesus' teaching relating to traumatic events can also be traced in Revelation.

Revelation picks up much Old Testament imagery, so it is also not surprising that it mirrors both Noah and Job. The final universal judgement mirrors the first universal judgement, and, like Genesis 6-9, emphasizes God's control of both human wickedness and the natural order.[14] The imagery of storms is frequent: for example, Jesus has a voice like mighty waters (1.15), the throne emits thunder and lightning (4.5) but is encircled by a rainbow (4.3).

Throughout, Revelation reassures of God's control and of the ultimate safety of his people. It is important to note that these two areas are the focus of worship for both human beings and the heavenly hosts throughout. The vision of God's throne (chapters 4 and 5) which is foundational to the whole book, indicates his control over both the natural order and over human sin. In chapter 4, God is worshipped for his supremacy in creation (4.11). In chapter 5, the slain Lamb appears beside the throne, and receives worship because his death has dealt with sin (v9-10). It is this dealing with human wickedness that offers safety and empowerment to those who believe. It follows that, to be assured of safety in the midst of cosmic upheaval, we need to know that the rule of God, which supercedes all earthly rule, is also the rule of his Christ (11.15); and that the 'Lord of lords and King of kings' who is the judging warrior who puts a final end to human wickedness (19.16) is also the Lamb who has made safe the faithful (17.14).

There is, then, much in Revelation that speaks into traumatic experience. Here, I shall offer some brief pointers structured around the themes of Jesus' teaching in Matthew 24, Mark 13 and Luke 21.

TRAUMATIC EVENTS ARE TO BE EXPECTED

Revelation certainly normalizes trauma. It reassures the church that these things will happen, and that we need to be prepared for them in order to stand through them. Like Job, Revelation gives much space to natural disasters, and deals with questions of justice and of the worthiness and worship of God. Like the Noah story, it has to do with God's un-making and re-making his world in response to human wickedness.

14 It is interesting to compare and contrast the two judgements. One has the salvation of one family in the ark; the other the salvation of countless thousands through the blood of Christ. One is a single cataclysm that destroys all; the other a series of deliberately limited judgements that offers opportunity for repentance. One is followed by the re-creation of the world to accommodate wickedness and death; the other culminates in a new creation which excludes wickedness and death.

TRAUMATIC EVENTS ARE MEANINGFUL

Like Job, Revelation addresses the question of trauma on earth in the light of what is going on in heaven. In particular, it recognizes the dimension of Satanic activity. It represents Satan as the enemy of humans, especially of believers, and also as the enemy of God. It goes much further than Job, seeing Satan's activity in terms of warfare, and announcing his ultimate defeat. The believer's part in this warfare is potentially martyrdom, but certainly witness (12.11 cf. 1.9). As in Jesus' teaching, the traumatic events find their meaning in relation to the establishment of the Kingdom of God. An added focus of Revelation is that the events are associated throughout with humans and angels worshipping the King.

As Job's comforters asserted, and as in the flood, the traumatic events are also seen as judgements. They are part of the sovereign Lord's cleaning up of His creation, and it is this aspect of them that provokes the grand worship of chapter 19. As is clear from chapter 16, the seven 'bowls of God's wrath' (v1) are also a call to repentance, but, sadly, one that is not heeded (v9, 11).

TRAUMATIC EVENTS ARE LIMITED

Like Job, Revelation climaxes with the appearance of God. While Job has only the voice of God in the whirlwind, Revelation has, quite literally, heaven coming down. While Job's personal suffering comes to an end after his encounter with God, all suffering comes to an end as heaven comes down and every tear is wiped away (21.4). From beginning to end, there is assurance that the end will come 'soon' (1.1, 22.20). Two thousand years on, we may wonder what 'soon' means; but at least it indicates that God's timing will be right.

THERE IS SOMETHING THAT WILL NEVER PASS AWAY.

Like Job, Revelation takes us to the throne of God. Behind all the events on earth is the sovereign God in heaven, and the Alpha and Omega who is alive for evermore. The vision of God's throne in chapters 4 and 5 is helpful here. We note the potentially destructive and terrifying thunder and lightning that has its origin in the throne itself (4.5), but that is preceded by the rainbow that surrounds the throne and reminds us of God's covenant with Noah (4.3). The traumatic events described in the later chapters are not only under God's control, but also subject to his commitment to humankind.

It is not surprising, then, that we find in these chapters both the sacrifice and the pain in the heart of God. The elder informs John that the Lion of Judah has conquered: John looks and sees the Lamb – the symbol of sacrifice; and this Lamb has been slain. The slaying, the wounding, of the Lamb, is stated three times (5.6, 9, 12). It is the slaying that makes him worthy to open the scroll and to be worshipped. It is also the slaying that opens the mission to all tribes and peoples. Here then is the completion of the Noah story.

THOSE WHO ENDURE TO THE END WILL BE SAFE

Revelation declares that there is ultimate safety available for those who persevere through the trauma, as well as for those who repent in response to it. The saints who go through the traumatic events will be safe in the presence of God (7.15-17). The survivors of the earthquake of chapter 11 are terrified, but they praise God (11.13).

The corollary, often unwelcome to Western Christian ears, is that those who do not endure, or who do not repent, will not be safe. As observed above, one of the purposes of the traumatic events is to give a final call to repentance. In trying to avoid the errors of Job's comforters, we may stop people, including ourselves, from hearing this call, and forget that Job's route to peace included repentance (Job 42.6). The exact meaning here is difficult to ascertain, but the symbolism of 'dust and ashes' certainly implies a measure of humbling, and of Job's learning to see himself in a right perspective (cf. Genesis 18.27). As the letters to the churches in Revelation 2 and 3 make clear, traumatic events can be calls to change for believers as well as for unbelievers.

4. Biblical Resources 2: Reconnection

4.1 Job again

Reconnection is hard for the traumatised person because it is a re-introduction of oneself to the world, and the self has been through disconnection and fragmentation. There are two implications here. First, the reconnecting self is not quite the same as the self that the world knew before. She functions differently, looks at the world differently, and relates to God in a whole new way. Perhaps the most challenging and painful aspect of reconnection is that she understands herself differently, and it can take a long time for others to recognize the person she now thinks she is. Second, as has already been observed, the three stages of recovery are not discrete. The person attempting to reconnect with the outside world is likely to be still going through the process of reconnecting the inner fragments. She is therefore still needing to process memories, and is vulnerable to any response from the world that her being may interpret as linked with the trauma. Reconnecting with the world can feel like returning to a place of great danger.

The last chapter of Job is instructive here. The book has spent forty chapters on Job's reconnection with God and with himself: now **God helps Job to reconnect to others**.

Having faced himself and his troubles in his meeting with God, he is not just left to sort out his relationships with comforters, friends and family, and to re-establish his business. God does it for him.

- God speaks to the comforters, and vindicates Job.
- He sends the comforters to Job, rather than making Job take the difficult step of confronting them.
- He gives Job an important task, and then honours it.
- He restores what has been lost.

> I shall always be grateful for the people who helped my father to make connections in the UK, and who were, for us, the extended family that we would not otherwise have had.

The book of Job has a happy ending in this life – the happiest ending that the writer could imagine at that stage in history. But I do not think that reconnection was finished with the restoration of Job's fortunes. The final stage was the writing of the story, leaving a public record for all to see. This final stage is important in that it affirms Job's being and the value of his experience. The memory matters. It is also the way in which future generations, like us, can receive its blessing: the passing on of the story gives it a significance for all time, that makes the whole experience worthwhile.

4.2 Celebrating survival

> And Moses said to the people: 'Remember this day on which you went free from Egypt, the house of bondage, how the Lord freed you from it with a mighty hand.' (Exodus 13.3)

A key to recovery from trauma is recognition that you have survived, and that survival is good. Both of these can be problematic for those who suffer 'survivor guilt'. The Bible's celebrations of survival can be of great help here. I have found myself singing, 'I'm alive, I'm alive, I'm alive for evermore – Jesus is risen from the dead!' and it's some years since I concluded that the single most significant theological insight on the holocaust is that the 'final solution' failed – and we are here to prove it.

At the heart of Christian identity is the celebration of the resurrection, which is not only Jesus' survival of crucifixion but also the proof that his trauma was eternally worthwhile. Revelation rings with the assurance that he was dead, but is alive for evermore (1.18). The resurrection offers the believer personal assurance of eternal survival, even though the horror of 'it happening again' should occur.

At the heart of Jewish identity is the celebration of the Passover, which is not only the history of the formation of a people, but also a celebration of survival and migration.

The very first thing Moses is recorded as saying to the Israelites after they left Egypt is 'Remember this day'. They are still in a state of extreme danger – more than 600,000 people in the desert, with limited provisions (12.39), and Pharaoh is about to send his troops after them, and Moses stops to tell them, 'Remember this day'. He adds an educational programme for coming generations (13.8, 9, 14, 16). Remembrance, it seems, takes priority over provision and even escape for flourishing after survival. Remembrance of what? Of THIS day – the day of freedom, and not the centuries of bondage. Of course, the Passover festival continues to recount the trauma, but, for the long term, the identity that is being established prioritises survival over trauma: 'We were slaves . . . this is what we suffered . . . but God brought us out.'

A second biblical festival, *Purim* also celebrates the survival of a migrant people, this time of a minority threatened with violent extinction. If we may stray outside the Bible, we might add *Hanukah*, with its dimension of survival in the face of a political and cultural domination that threatened worship. These three festivals ritualise the regular processing of communal traumatic memories, giving them meaning and enabling the community to place them in the past without losing them, thus allowing them to form identity in a positive manner.

This suggests to me that Scripture is teaching us to transform memories of trauma into celebrations of survival. Iconic for me personally is 'Holocaust Memorial Day' - January 27th, which happens to be my birthday. I have always tried to avoid the lugubrious media reminders of the horrors, which tend but to revive the agony. Can I make the day instead into a celebration of my, and our, existence? It is, after all, the anniversary of the **liberation** of Auschwitz.

The book of Revelation makes me pause here and ask whether I am being too Jewish. It has no celebration of a particular people, but of all peoples together around the throne of God. Perhaps the United States 'melting pot' model is nearer to this than the United Kingdom 'salad bowl' which celebrates ethnic distinction. But the gathered nations around the throne still have their languages, and the Americans are a gathering of migrant peoples, many with traumatic histories. They are liberated slaves, escapees from threatened destruction and political oppression . . . all with a history of survival to celebrate.

But peoples come and go. Does the history of peoples really matter in eternal terms? If, as I believe, Israel is an icon of humanity, the answer has to be 'Yes.' God chose to work through a family and a people rather than through, say, a series of prophets. Israel is special, and not all peoples have four thousand years of memories to celebrate, but all have something they have survived.

5. No mission without trauma?

We finish, as we began, with the links between trauma and mission. It is, perhaps, obvious by now that mission may involve ministry to the traumatized, particularly if it is in the context of migration. We have also explored Jesus' warning in Matthew 24, Mark 13 and Luke 21, that missionaries need to be prepared for traumatic events that result either from persecution or from the circumstances in which they will work. However, the juxtaposition of mission with traumatic events in these chapters makes me ask whether there is a more fundamental link. Is trauma some how NECESSARY to mission?

This paper is part of my own movement towards 'reconnection as a survivor' – my celebration of survival not as a diminished thing still suffering from traumatic symptoms and with a 'working memory' a shadow of its former self, but as an augmented person, with something new to offer to the Body of Christ. I can see the trauma as preparation for the next stage of the mission to which God has called me. Perhaps I am not alone. Perhaps a measure of trauma, or, at least, the experience of traumatic events, is a necessary equipment for mission.

Jesus' own instructions about mission in Matthew 10 and Luke 10 begin by telling the disciples to take nothing with them. How, we wonder, can we even begin to follow this pattern in the twenty first century? Moving into new communities and different countries, we are usually required to bring things with us – not only for our own sustenance, but so as to contribute something to the receiving community. How can we achieve the stripping of self that makes us dependent on the hospitality of those to whom we proclaim the Gospel? One way is arriving as refugees. For the rest of us, who do not have this privilege, perhaps the experience of trauma is one way, for it is rooted in helplessness.

The books speak of the need to EMPOWER the trauma victim – to replace the sense of helplessness with a sense of control. I have argued instead for the sense that we are small, but that God is in control. What about power? What kind of sense of power does the survivor need, especially if she is to be an effective missionary? Jesus, who has power over winds and waves, systematically refused the obvious power of material goods, political status and wrong use of the miraculous throughout his ministry. The way to resurrection power was, for him, a very literal stripping and wounding. As the Septuagint helpfully translates Isaiah 53.5, 'He was traumatized for our transgressions.' Trauma is necessary to mission, because there is pain in the heart of God.

And that brings us back to the theme of worship. I have said that we cannot tell, from the book of Job, the tone of the voice from the whirlwind; but we do know that Job was satisfied and worshipped. The book of Revelation makes things much more clear: from the first vision of Jesus, through the worship around the throne, and to the final vision of heaven, we see the traumatized and risen Messiah at the heart of God. It is he who is the first revelation to the exiled John, and who says, 'Do not fear!' and 'I know... I know... I know... I know... I know... I know... I know.' (1.17; 2.2, 9, 13, 19; 3.1, 8,15). It is he, who is the missionary and the survivor, who is in control (1.5).

The traumatized are invited, then, to worship. It is not enough to know that God is in control: we are invited to be glad that he is in control, to address him, to enter into relationship with him. Like Job, we can acknowledge his greatness and our smallness as we respond to his coming to us. Like John, we can fall down before the crucified. As we worship, we will find that worship is actually something needed for recovery, because we need to reconnect to God in order to reconnect to ourselves and to the world. Worship puts life into perspective: it enables us to take the focus off the traumatized self, and to focus on the traumatized Messiah. As we face our ongoing vulnerability and the fact that we will never be the same again, we recognize the scars that remained after the resurrection and the ascention into heaven. Those scars tell us that Jesus' trauma accomplished something – that he is now our Safe Place.

And that brings us back to mission. Why was the Messiah traumatized? To ransom not only us, but also people from every tribe and language and people and nation (Revelation 5.9). It is this that provokes the worship of heaven. Let us, then, end with the instructions given by the Master as he faces his own coming trauma, and prepares his disciples for theirs:

Matthew 24 gives the basics:

- watch out; be ready (v 4, 42-44);
- don't be alarmed (v6);
- keep loving (v12);
- stand firm (v13);
- don't be deceived (v4, 23-6);
- at the right time, flee (v16-18);
- pray (v20).

Mark 13 adds instructions for mission: Don't worry about what to say: say what is given to you, for it will be the Holy Spirit who speaks through you (Mark 13.11). Luke 21 makes it very personal – the persecution will be because of Jesus, and he himself promises to give words and wisdom (v12-17).

Expect traumatic events, says our Lord. Be ready for them, so that you can take your part in God's mission to his world of pain. If we face traumatic events in this way, will we be spared the wounding? Perhaps not, but we can be sure of our place in the Kingdom of God. 'Not a hair of your head will perish. By standing firm, you will gain life' (Luke 21.18-19).

Biographical Information:

Until recently, Dr Ida Glaser was Senior Teaching and Research Fellow at The Edinburgh Centre for Muslim-Christian Studies. She also has experience of teaching physics in Islamic contexts and of church-based outreach in multi-racial, inner-city Britain. Employed by Crosslinks, she was the director of Faith to Faith, a Christian consultancy on other faiths. She is the Academic Director of the new Oxford Centre for Muslim-Christian Studies.